Putting My Stuff in the Past

Healing *and* Reconciliation

Willie Eugene Marshall

authorHOUSE®

AuthorHouse™
1663 Liberty Drive
Bloomington, IN 47403
www.authorhouse.com
Phone: 1 (800) 839-8640

Published by AuthorHouse   10/19/2015

ISBN: 978-1-5049-5596-6 (sc)
ISBN: 978-1-5049-5595-9 (e)

Print information available on the last page.

This book is printed on acid-free paper.

Scripture quotations marked KJV are from the Holy Bible, King James Version (Authorized Version). First published in 1611. Quoted from the KJV Classic Reference Bible, Copyright © 1983 by The Zondervan Corporation.

PRAISE FOR PUTTING MY STUFF IN THE PAST

"Thank you Dr. W.E. Marshall for following God's directions in writing and publishing this Work Study Book. As Christians, we all "must" *get past* "all" hindrances, stumbling blocks, greed, envy, and pride, then reconcile with one another to be healed by God!"

-Dr. Jo Ann Sumbry

Pastor, Educational Leader, Professional Consultant, and Co-Author of *Mother and Son: A Book of Poems and Other Writings*

I first met Dr. Marshall in 2013 in the holding area of the operating room at my hospital where he was having surgery for a devastating left upper extremity injury from a motor vehicle accident. I helped to take care of him. On top post rounds, the next morning he asked about my church and family while enduring pain. Even a life altering injury couldn't deter him from his positive witness. That was the being of our friendship through texting. I really believe that this healing and reconciliation Work Study Book will be a great piece that will help people all over the world both in the areas of physical and spiritual healing. Dr. Marshall is the most positive person I have ever met.

-Fran Boyette, M.D.

Montgomery, AL

This theological and practical tool is just what the church needs.

Derick D. Dailey

Yale University, M.A.R. (2014)

Global Ecumenical Theological Institute

World Council of Churches

Fordham University School of Law J.D. Candidate 2017

Dr. Willie Marshall has produced a tool that will be effective in dismantling the golden "elephant that has been in the room" far too long in the body of Christ. This honest and comprehensive workbook will assist clergy and lay in the praxis of restoration and reconciliation. Thank your Dr. Marshall for exemplifying the utilization of faith, theological and psychological resources to provide practical remedies for pervasive issues that have infected the Church for centuries.

Dr. Cassandra Gould

Pastor, Quinn Chapel A.M.E. Church

Executive Director of Missouri Faith Voices

and Founder of Women of the Cloth

Dr. Marshall, it is with profound gratitude that I would like to thank you for sharing your wisdom and years of experience on relevant topics that has for too long been ignored. Thank you for creating conversation and thought provoking relevancy. Your book is much needed.

-John Lewis Dees, Jr.

Pastor, Emanuel African Methodist Episcopal Church

Mobile, AL

Dr. Marshall is a man of God who deeply cares about showing people the love of Jesus Christ. His concern is expressed in this work-book which can be used by churches both big or small. The information is all transferable in easy to read language. I praise God for this wonderful treasure that if read and utilized should be a blessing to the church.

-Dr. Robert Richard Allen Turner
Pastor, St. Paul African Methodist Episcopal Church
Tuscaloosa, AL

Honest, simple, direct...refreshing even. Prepare for your blessing! I was so incredibly enriched by this much needed work. On the surface, it would appear that Dr. Marshall and I met by circumstance that day on our flight, but it is more than clear that this was ordained by God. Over the years he has provided much needed encouragement and mentoring- always on time. THAT is what makes me certain that he is Spirit led. The Kingdom of our Lord will most certainly be blessed by not only reading but taking the time to understand the contents of this work. This is a solid work that addresses some tough subjects but is a MUST HAVE for church leaders and Christians as a whole.

-Alisha Thompson Congress, DO
Family Medicine Physician
Bessemer, AL

Hurt is a reality of life. We all experience this emotion at some point. Our past hurts can surely affect our present and our future productivity. We must evaluate ourselves along with our past situations honestly. Facing our past hurts, ask the Lord for healing and move forward. Thereafter, we will be able to serve as effective leaders, building the kingdom of God with compassion and genuine concern for our sisters and brothers. I highly recommend this work by Dr. Willie E. Marshall as a valuable tool in helping us to leave our past hurts behind us as we move forward in leading productive lives.

READ AND DIGEST WELL

-Dwight E. Dillard

Presiding Elder Birmingham-Florence-Tuscaloosa District
Northwest Alabama Conference

Dr. Marshall, thank you for sharing your thoughts, experiences and especially for ministering to both the laity and clergy in this book. Your observations are on point and help us to objectively see much of the hidden hurt that stifles both personal and spiritual growth. I am thankful to have watched your ministry grow and to see God's kingdom expand as you allow Him to use the gift He has anointed you with for the good of our Zion.

-Lamar P. Higgins

Board of Trustees
Troy University
Troy, AL

I recently had the good fortune of reading your material. It was well-written and contained sound, practical advice. In fact, I have already benefited from your discussion on church hurt. Dr. Marshall pointed out several things that I will remember for years to come. I look forward for your work touching hearts of all God's people. Thank you.

-Dr. C.P. Shears
Pastor, Saint Andrew Baptist Church
Jacksonville, FL.

Dr. Marshall, I've had the great fortune to have you as my Pastor and to serve in leadership for our church. You are a man of God who is filled with the spirit of positivity and have a heart for sharing God's Word. Your book is yet another example of giving back to the Body of Christ by providing useful tools to aid His people during times of hurt. Stay Positive!

-Dr. Michael D. Ward
Chair Pro-Tem, St. James African Methodist Episcopal Church
Board of Stewards
St. Louis, MO

In his book titled: "The Wounded Healer: Ministry in Contemporary Society", the distinguished theologian Henri Nouwen addresses the task of articulating the "predicament of the minister" after he/ she has been stripped of the traditional protection of their office. In an effort to render service to a hurting society, the minister is met with the additional challenge of managing the hurts and wounds of their own lives. To be sure, the desired healing (needed in the context of the present-day) all but demands that there be proper analysis, storage and discarding of the "stuff" that eventually erodes from the inside out. With similar tone and effect, Dr. Marshall provides the reader of this workbook with an in-depth critical review of "the self"; thus liberating both the minister and those ministered to; providing all parties with the ability to proceed into the dawn of new ministry and new witness. I applauded Dr. Marshall for extending the literature and giving a fresh, relevant text to those called to do ministry in the sacred community.

T. Eric Nathan, M.Div.
Pastor, Grant Chapel African Methodist Episcopal Church
Birmingham, AL

To God be the glory for such an enlightening, timely, and on point study book. Your years of laboring in the vineyard has afforded your eyes to see, ears to hear, and heart to weep at how past hurts in the body of Christ has cause pain and division at an astounding rate...and in some cases beyond repair, unless those involved humble themselves and allow the Holy Spirit to do a total reconciliation makeover! This book is a must have for "every member" in the body of Christ! Thank you Dr. Marshall for harking to the voice of God and charging forward in writing it. It's a blessing and will truly help us all in our walk with Christ!

Perry Stallworth, M.S.
Education Services Specialist - Department of Defense
Montgomery, AL

This divine work study book that Dr. Marshall created, addresses the human being most pressing concerns- their inalienable rights to the kingdom of God. The manuscript shows that you have the right to move from a place of hurt to happiness. I believe that this manuscript will touch countless amount of Christians as well as other faiths. Through effective communication all things can be solved. This manuscript shows the importance of how communication heals. Dr. Marshall whom I have grown to know and constantly admire has constantly shown me that he is a man of God as well as consistently enthusiastic in the fulfillment of God purpose. I appreciate and love Dr. Marshall (Rev) like a big brother and thankful for his contribution to humanity.

-Ronald L. Lewis

Barber and *Author of the Great work 7 principles.*

St. Louis, MO

Dr. Marshall, this work study book is truly amazing and inspiring. It not only gives insight from a laymen viewpoint but it also provides a prospective of how things are perceived from the pulpit. Dr. Marshall's work is really God sent masterpiece and it is sure to guide the reader in a positive direction. As a result of reading this document, I am committed to using the concepts he has discussed in my daily life to help me become a better person, brother, man, father, leader, follower and servant of Jesus Christ. Dr. Marshall, please keep up the good work and continue to be a blessing to others as they are a blessing to you.

Myron E. King
Fire Service Deputy Chief
Mobile Fire Rescue Department
Mobile, AL

FOREWORD

The challenges of serving in ministry in this age often leaves
many valuable people depleted of energy and enthusiasm.
The pain associated with unrealized breakthroughs, in
seasons of suffering, often presents uncomfortable dilemmas
for those who refuse to allow their faith to be shaken.
In this unique study book Dr. Willie E. Marshall provides
us with fresh and relevant ideas on how to "Get Past Our
Stuff". In this book Pastor Marshall helps us identify methods
and processes for moving from experiencing hurt to creating
healing in a manner that allows us to witness God at work.
This is the Study Book that many Pastors and Church Leaders have
been waiting for. A book which causes us to acknowledge our own
pain which in so many instances surfaces from our service and sacrifice
and at the same time work to move beyond that pain to the point we
can declare ourselves "healed" for the journey. In this Study Book
Dr. Marshall explores the all too often phenomenon of why churches,
laity and clergy hurt each other in a culture designed to help each.
Dr. Marshall's sensitive observations regarding the pain, problems
and pressures relating to Pastoral transition allows those who

have or will experience this journey the opportunity to encourage themselves through the application practical of faith principles. His thoughts regarding competition in the Kingdom encourages readers to come to grips with the unhealthy negative culture which has become so pervasive within the church and divides those whose mission ought to be "like minded". Through this writing Dr. Marshall presents a seasoned approach in viewing the autonomy of the local church while appreciating that church's connection to the concepts of being one in Christ.

In the chapter entitled People Releasing People, Dr. Marshall takes us to a cross road in growth which he's us explore the bittersweet issue of knowing when to let go and how to move forward. He permits us to be transparent in acknowledging that very often releasing others can be very difficult, even when it is very necessary. This Study Book offers us a method to objectively evaluate our attempt to grow in this area.

By including case studies within this Study Book helps readers to identify that we are not the, "only one who have traveled this road", allowing the reader to comfortably embrace the ideas offered within this guide.

PRAISE FOR PUTTING MY STUFF IN THE PAST: HEALING AND RECONCILIATION is a spiritually insightful and personally inspiring Study Book which effectively lays the groundwork for moving from hurting to healing. Kudos to Dr. Willie E. Marshall for tackling an area often ignored within the Body of Christ. Thank you for encouraging us to know that we can live Healed.

-Dr. Harold Mayberry
Senior Pastor, First AME Church
Oakland, CA

PREFACE

Infinite individuals are living with illnesses, with injuries, and with infections. They need to be seen by a physician to receive professional help. They do not want to go to the doctor to be examined because they are afraid the sickness may require surgery. So, they keep it to themselves. They try to treat it themselves. As a result, they become progressively worse. They discover that hiding the hurt does not bring healing.

The author exposes the epidemic of infinite individuals in the Christian Community who are living with illnesses, injuries, and infections. All of these can be identified by "*hurt*." The hurt is being harbored, hoarded, and housed in the heart.

We discover hiding the hurt does not bring healing.

We need to be seen by a physician to receive professional help. This is what the author offers in this work. He, literally, make us an appointment to be seen by the Great Physician who can diagnose our hurt, prescribe the treatment, and schedule the therapy that will bring us healing.

We hold on to the hurt because we are afraid of the healing process. The uncertainty of what we will have to go through and what we will need to have done causes us to hold on to the hurt. The unknown responses and the unpredictable reactions cause us to hold on to the hurt. Both, clergy and congregants, have experienced hurt, either, *in* the ministry, *by* the members, or *with* the move. Healing must be found because it is hard to work while wounded. It is difficult to have harmony while hurting. It is difficult to worship while warring. For these reasons, the author is rushing us to the Emergency Room of our Ecumenical Relationships to Enter Relief and to Embrace Reconciliation.

This book "Putting Your Stuff in the Past," is a Therapy Session, a Treatment Schedule, a True Solution, a Top Surgeon, and a Trusted Source for the threatening sickness, tormenting soreness, and traumatizing syndrome that the author identifies as "*hurt.*" This product is a prescription that has been tested by the truth and approved by the medical board of mediating believers and is guaranteed to cure the hurt caused by the conflicts, the confrontations, and the competitions in the Church. We are indebted to the author for highlighting the healing for our hurt and for revealing the remedy for our reconciliation.

-Dr. Jeffrey T. Rainey
Pastor, Christian Union Primitive Baptist Church
Mobile, Alabama

DEDICATION

I would like to dedicate this Work Study Book to my awesome St. James African Methodist Episcopal Church family in St. Louis, Missouri and all of the pastoral congregations and communities, I have been privileged to serve.

I dedicate this book to my mentor, Dr. Homer McCall, Sr., who has helped me greatly through my ministry and in my life with authentic and seasoned guidance.

To all of the Episcopal Leadership of the African Methodist Episcopal Church, I have had the privilege to serve under, Bishop Frank Madison Reid, Jr., Bishop Cornelius Egbert Thomas, Bishop Zedekiah Lazett Grady, Bishop Theodore Larry Kirkland and Bishop James Levert Davis.

I also dedicate this book to my wonderful J.F. Shields high school class of 1983, Beatrice, AL.

To my late father Presiding Elder James Marshall, my mother Lucy R. Watts-Marshall who are the greatest encouragers I have ever known to exist on planet earth and to all of my family and friends.

To my loving wife Kimberly and my gifted son Joshua. Thank you for all your continued encouragement and support. I love you dearly!

Stay Positive!

Contents

INTRODUCTION

This work study book is designed to help clergy and laity all over the world to find effective ways to deal with and eventually move beyond the hurt and pain, "the stuff" of their past through a "positive" process of healing and reconciliation before they find themselves as hurting people hurting other people. Everybody goes through something regardless of who they are. Therefore, we never know when people are going through their stuff. Nobody is exempt from pain and hurt. As we have heard many people say, "Church hurt is the worst hurt," but in my opinion "hurt is hurt wherever it occurs." I would like to address church hurt, healing and reconciliation both in the pulpit and in the pew focusing on the following: church hurt, the pastor and the pastor's family, the impact of the itinerancy, competition in the kingdom, rebuilding the trust and people releasing people.

In *"The Peace Maker: A Biblical Guide to Resolving Personal Conflict,"* Ken Sande writes: It is impossible to truly forgive others in your own strength, especially when they have hurt you deeply or betrayed your trust. You can try not to think about what they did or stuff your feelings deep inside and put on a false smile when you see them. But unless your heart is cleansed and changed by God, the

memories and the feelings will still be lurking in the background, poisoning your thoughts and words and preventing the rebuilding of trust and relationship.

The church, God's house, is still the best place for us as a modern day kingdom building family. I must highly stress that God's church is perfect because He made it but we as living individuals are fallible people and do make mistakes. The objective of this book is not to simply reveal the errors that we as clergy and laity fall into by hurting each other but to deal with the crucial issues in the room, not just continuing to patch up our old and fresh wounds but to find healing prescriptions to help both clergy and laity become more effective, healthy and kingdom minded disciples for this work called ministry. If we don't consistently deal with the problems then the chronic problems of hurt, lack of healing and reconciliation will continue to gradually destroy us on all levels from the inside out. If you have been hurt and you still haven't gotten past the pain of your past then there is no better time than right now to start putting your stuff in the past. "Stay Positive," on the mark, get set, let's go:

1. Admit to yourself and to God you need to begin a process of healing and reconciliation as a result of your hurt and pain.
2. Forgive yourself and the other person who inflicted the hurt and pain on you. (Leave it at the altar).
3. Then ask God to continue to help you to heal and reconcile taking one day at a time.

CHAPTER 1

Church Hurt

How then shall they call on him in whom they have not believed? And how shall they believe in him of whom they have not heard? And how shall they hear without a preacher? And shall they preach, except they be sent? As it is written, how beautiful are the feet of them that preach the gospel of peace, and bring glad tiding of good things! For they have not all obeyed the gospel. For Esaias saith, Lord, who hath believed our report? So then faith cometh by hearing and hearing by the word of God.

-Romans 10:14-17

But if we walk in the light, as he is in the light, we have fellowship one with another, and the blood of Jesus Christ his Son cleanseth us from all sin.

– John 1:7

Clergy Hurting Clergy

The more we as clergy work together for the good of the kingdom, get to know and understand each other the more we can peacefully share and resolve our indifferences without tearing one another down. As a result, we will be able to grow more in God's grace, decrease the percentage of clergy hurting clergy and become more kingdom focused working together because we all really need each other.

Dearly beloved, avenge not yourselves, but rather give place unto wrath: for it is written, Vengeance is mine: I will repay, saith the Lord.

-Romans 12:19

Clergy Hurting Laity

In simple terms, sometimes even we as pastors can let our egotistical ecclesiastical privileges blow our heads up and as a result we will find ourselves whether intentionally or unintentionally hurting laity. I know some laypersons have lost their minds, into pastoral mode and can be extremely hard to work with but it's still absolutely no excuse for clergy to abuse laity. In such a case there should be enough spiritual maturity from both clergy and laity to agree to disagree and have ample wisdom to do what is best for the overall church. We as clergy must never develop acute or chronic stages of amnesia; forgetting that without God sent laity our pews will be empty in many ways. On the other hand, laity must also know and understand that they can't hear the word without a God sent preacher.

Laity Hurting Clergy

God didn't call laity to pastor or to abuse the pastor but only to serve as lay leaders in the house of God. There must be a healthy working relationship between the laity and clergy and not creative ways to hurt the pastor for power and control. Even though a layperson may have been hurt by another clergy person it doesn't give the right to hurt somebody else.

In the words of the late Rodney King, "Can we all just get along?"

Laity Hurting Laity

One of the other unfortunate quarrels of division in the church is when laity can't get along with laity. Sometimes just like all other levels of hurts this unhealed and unreconciled process most of the time filtered from the outside of the church into the inside. This type of behavior can overflow into the hearts of people hindering the spiritual growth of the individual as well as the church. Such unresolved poison of laity hurting laity can cause a person to leave the church and possibly never go to church again.

Case Study

Layperson J shared in how she was really hurt by several laypersons in her local church. Layperson J also stated that in certain events she was overwhelmed how laity in the church who she looked up to would make her feel as though she didn't have the same the worth, not welcome and excluded from feeling as though she was a part of the church family. Layperson J struggles with understanding how people can be self-righteous in the midst of their wrongs and it's accepted. Layperson J discovered when she got older that there was so much bias, mean cliques and division in the church. Whenever Layperson J leadership program wouldn't be successful instead of other laity genuinely supporting her they would destructively criticize her to other people in the church and in the community.

As a result, Layperson J feel hurt, hesitant to ask others for help, she felt bad, and neglected. Because of layperson J's love for God and ministry she hasn't allowed the behaviors of other laity to break her walk with God. She stated that she has grown even more because of this shocking episode. She hasn't after about five years confronted these persons but she has forgiven them, still love, speak to them and pray for them even though it still hurts to a certain degree.

Self-Growth Evaluation Questions

1. As clergy have you ever inflicted hurt on another clergy or been a victim yourself of hurt from another clergy and how did this make you feel?
2. Did you and the other clergyperson ever heal and reconcile beyond the hurt of this situation?
3. As clergy have you ever hurt any layperson and how did this make you feel?
4. Did you as clergy and Layperson ever heal and reconcile beyond the hurt of this situation?
5. As laity have you ever hurt a clergyperson? How did you feel after you hurt this clergyperson?
6. Did you and this clergyperson ever heal and reconcile from the hurt of this situation?
7. As a layperson have you ever been hurt by another layperson and how did this make you feel?
8. Did you ever heal and reconcile with the other layperson?

Answer Sheet

_____

_____

_____

_____

_____

_____

_____

_____

_____

_____

_____

_____

_____

_____

_____

_____

_____

_____

_____

_____

_____

_____

_____

_____

_____

CHAPTER 2

The Impact of the Itineracy

Norman Shawchuck and Roger Heuser, in their book *Managing the Congregation*, wrote the following about unresolved conflicts: "Unmanaged conflict frays nerves and wears down persons' patience until finally, all ministries of the church grind to a halt. Some persons fight to the finish; others break their ties with the congregation and go elsewhere."

How Moving Affects the Pastor and Family Moving from One Church to Another Church

Often times the moving or the itinerant process is only focused on the hurt and pain of the congregation and not on the hurt and pain of the pastor and the pastor's family. When they move to another church this shifting cause pain and hurt for them as well because of the relationships established with others. We often fail to admit that this congregation has also become a part of the pastor and pastor's family. This phase of ministry must be handled with extreme care so that there will be a healthy move for the pastor and family leaving and for the new pastor and family who is coming in to serve the church.

How It Affects the Local Congregation

When a pastor and their family moves to another church especially if there is a good personality matching rapport between the both of them it can be a really hurtful transition. This moving process can actually affect a congregation in several ways such as:

1. Not being able to accept the reality of the present pastor and family.
2. Not being able to make the adjustment in terms of accepting the new pastor and family.
3. Wrestling with the psychological warfare of actually staying at their church because the person can't handle the change of new leadership. As a result, all parties are affected in one way or another.

Case Study

Clergy X shared that moving from one church to another church affected his family in numerous ways. Financially, it took a toll on his family because they had to leave jobs, and had to relocate and establish a life in a different location. However, it has brought them closer together and increased their faith in God.

When they left their previous local congregation, the affect was that they were initially for the most part sad, frustrated or confused as to why the move had to take place. Some did not attend church for a while, others bounce back rather quickly. One of clergy X biggest fears was ministries that were organized may or may not be continued depending on the relationship and vision of the newly assigned pastor and family.

Therefore, clergy X wisely advice others who are in this itinerant ministry, to own your house so that you will always have some where to go whenever you need. Also, ensure you obtain some type of health insurance because most small to medium size churches do not offer health insurance. Lastly, value your family time, your time, and personal space and make sure your congregation knows it because when it is all said and done your family came with you to the church and your family will be the one leaving with you when it is time to go. Trust in God when even when you may not trust in the church, in the denomination or even in their leadership.

Self-Growth Evaluation Questions

1. As a pastor serving a local church in what way did it affect you when you left that church and moved to another church?

2. As the family of the pastor in what ways did it affect you when you had to move to a new congregation?

3. How do you think the congregation felt after the pastor and his family left? How did the congregation handle it and what's your relationship with that congregation as of today?

4. As a layperson in a local church having experienced a pastor or pastors moving from your church to another church, how did the moving process in your opinion affect you as well as the local congregation?

5. Have you as a pastor, the pastor's family or as a local layperson been able to move on as a result of the overall process of changing pastors and moving from one church to another church?

Answer Sheet

CHAPTER 3

Competition in the Kingdom

And James and John, the sons of Zebedee, come unto him, saying, Master, we would that thou shouldest do for us whatsoever we shall desire. And he said unto them, what would ye that I should do for you? They said unto him, Grant unto us that we may sit, one on thy right hand, and the other on thy left hand, in thy glory. But Jesus said unto them, ye know not what ye ask: can ye drink of the cup that I drink of? And be baptized with the baptism that I am baptized with? And they said unto him, we can. And Jesus said unto them, ye shall indeed drink of the cup that I drink of; and with the baptism that I am baptized withal shall ye be baptized: But to sit on my right hand and on my left hand is not mine to give; but it shall be given to them for whom it is prepared. And when the ten heard it, they began to be much displeased with James and John.

-Mark 10:35-41

Clergy and Laity

Believe it or not there is a high level of unholy competition in the church between clergy and clergy, clergy and laity, and laity and laity on all levels which has caused wounded discord in the church family. There isn't anything wrong with, in my opinion, being competitive in a godly way because we all want to be good at what God has called us to do for His kingdom. Through my 28 years of pastoral experience there is just something about some clergy and laity having an addiction to this vehicle called "control," "being in charge," one trying to compete with the other one. The brother has to have the "remote" and the sister has to have the "last word" mentality which has caused major conflict in the church among both clergy and laity. This kind of competitive behavior when observed by others can be a major turn off crippling the individual's authentic walk with God along with the spiritual growth of others shifting from a true God sent focus. These types of activities give a negative persona of both clergy and laity implementing high levels of spiritual immaturity that can inflict insecurity, dislikes, jealousy, grudges, being an opportunist, wanting to be the star and out front to be seen for selfish gain, and lack of unified camaraderie.

Case Study

Clergy V states, competition can be good or bad depending on its context. However, when it comes to ministry, there should be no competition. The Bible tells us in 1 Peter 4:10, that we should use whatever gifts we have received to serve others and to faithfully administer God's grace in its various forms. God created each of us in a unique way. It is this distinction that allows me to do things that no one can do quite like me. It is for that reason that a spirit of competition is an exercise in futility that results in a negative impact to Kingdom building as these events are viewed by others.

My personal experiences regarding church competition are varied. I've encountered ridicule and competitive jealousy which initially made me uncomfortable. Those experiences pushed me into a position of either taking flight or fight. As I reflect, I now understand that they were stepping stones God used to develop me into the person that I am. They also taught me how to minister to others who may experience similar situations. What I considered a negative was actually a positive. It helped me to become more compassionate in preparation for Kingdom service.

It's my observation that competition in church/ministry has a negative impact on others. All one must do is take a look at how the world views church/ministry in the 21st century. We are to be salt and light. We are to attract those in the world to Jesus by our actions, beliefs and lifestyles. To operate in God's Kingdom in a spirit of competition is a worldly way. It weakens personal witness and confirms the church body as being hypocritical.

I would advise clergy to honestly examine themselves to understand the motivation behind doing the things that we do. Every minister should focus on being who God wants them to become. In doing so, they will achieve what God wants them to do for the Kingdom. Our service isn't about self, but the Savior. Competing with other ministers is a trap which hinders one from reaching their full potential and God's successful design for their life.

As for Laity, I would advise that they develop in true Christian character. Laity must study the word of God. They will gain an understanding of what true Christianity looks like and realize that competition in the body of Christ is a deception of the enemy. This deception damages the relationships that we as children of God must value for we serve a God of relationship.

Self-Growth Evaluation Questions

1. Have you ever seen clergy and laity in competition before?
2. Were you surprised and how did this make you feel?
3. How has clergy and laity competition affected your view of the ministry and of church in the 21st century?

Answer Sheet

CHAPTER 4

Rebuilding the Trust

Stephen Covey quotes, "Trust is the glue of life. It's the most essential ingredient in effective communication. It's the foundational principle that holds all relationships".

But seek ye first the kingdom of God, and his righteousness; and all these things shall be added unto you.

-Matthew 6:33

Restoration of Trust at the Table

Rebuilding our trust, as hard as it can be, requires starting afresh, letting go of the pain and hurt of the past. We must come together, sit at the table of reconciliation and collaborate through hearing each other milking out the rationale clarity, accepting the responsibility of whatever wrong we have inflicted on others and ourselves not pretending or playing the blame game. There has to be a mutual agreement among all parties to at least attempt to start the process of rebuilding the trust at the table so that healthy relationships can be restored. Because with God it is always possible to bring back the levels of trust that's needed in spite of the old and new wounds.

Case Study

In 2014 clergy A felt highly betrayed and disappointed by clergy B. Clergy A thought that called ministers could be trusted by other called ministers. Clergy A shared some personal and confidential information with clergy B and clergy A discovered that clergy B had exposed the information to other people. Of course, this was very shocking and hurting to clergy A and has caused clergy A to very careful how he shares any confidential information with other clergy.

As a result, clergy A finally forgave clergy B but mentioned how this experience has helped his ministry to grow to a level of forgiveness that clergy A didn't think he could do. Even though, it is still hard for him to trust other clergy because of this one incident.

<u>Self-Growth Evaluation Questions</u>

1. Have you ever been betrayed by a clergy or layperson?
2. How did it make you feel at the time?
3. Did you ever restore any level of trust with the person? If not, why haven't you as of yet?

Answer Sheet

CHAPTER 5

People Releasing People

And we know that all things work together for good to them that love God, to them who are the called according to *his* purpose.

-Romans 8:28

We all have to be very careful in this releasing or Exodus process that we follow the directions of God and not the directions only of our emotional hurt and pain. We must make sure that our releasing of others is in line with God's timing and not just our timing.

We Have to Release Ourselves

When we release ourselves, it can help us to be able to accept and have a better understanding of the overall releasing process that is for the good of all parties involved even if it's for a season or for a lifetime.

We Have to Release Others

As crazy as it may sound the reality is that in order for us to move forward to heal and reconcile in our lives there are some people we have to release out of our lives. This release stage may be only for a season or even a life time. Please don't misunderstand me this doesn't mean these persons are bad people, it only means they aren't designed to travel with you during this certain phase of life because they haven't been called by God to make the shift with you.

Other People Have to Release Us

Even some of our friends and family members have to release us in order for them to heal and reconcile beyond where they are in their walk with God. Sometimes there are places we can't go with them because we haven't been prepared by God to go to where they are going without being a hindrance to them. Some people will stay with us for a lifetime while others will stay only for a particular season. It is crucial that we make sure before we add too or put people out of our lives know that our process of Healing and Reconciliation is directly from God.

Case Study

Young adult layperson K shares the following information: Yes, I have had a few friends I had to release from my life, and the feeling is never good. It is actually very challenging for someone like myself, who always looks for the good in people. However, as I have grown over the years, I have learned time, situations and trials will make you aware of who is a genuine friend with your best interests in mind, and who is not. It's always important to surround yourself with those who genuinely care for you. But you have to realize you won't have a crowd of friends in the end, maybe just one or two who are there for a lifetime and not just a season.

I cannot think of a friend who has released me from their life, but I have noticed a mutual distance between myself and others. Distance where we don't hate one another, but know that we aren't meant to be close friends.

Currently, I am going through the process of trying to release a certain someone from my life, and it is challenging. I truly know that in order for me to progress further in life, I need to let this person go.

As a result, I think that all of our life experiences shape who we are. You truly live and learn each day. It is all to make us better. Every trial is meant to teach us certain things, and aid in our life's purpose. Today, I am still learning and growing. I am not perfect, and I know that no one is except God. So with that in mind, I know I will make mistakes, I will trust someone I shouldn't, but in the end, I know whoever the Lord places in my life has a purpose. It is up to me to recognize if it is for a season or a lifetime.

Self-Growth Evaluation Questions

1. Have you ever experienced releasing yourself before?
2. How did you feel as a result of someone releasing you?
3. Did you ever learn how to move on with your life in a positive way?
4. Have you ever experienced releasing others out of your life before?
5. As of today did God ever reveal to you the purpose for your releasing of yourself, your releasing of others and for others releasing of you?

Answer Sheet

_____

_____

_____

_____

_____

_____

_____

_____

_____

_____

_____

_____

_____

_____

_____

_____

_____

_____

_____

_____

_____

_____

_____

_____

_____

_____

_____

CONCLUSION

I truly hope and pray you have enjoyed reading and working through *"Putting My Stuff in the Past: Healing and Reconciliation Work Study Book" and* that you have benefited in some way from each chapter, the various case studies and the self-growth evaluation questions. Since all of us will encounter various types of hurt and pain it is my desire to encourage us to "Stay Positive" and start a process of getting better so that at the right time we can put our stuff in the past having consistent optimistic expectations.

Optimistic Expectations – is having so much faith in God, already speaking victory into the atmosphere even though you haven't seen the outcome as of yet.

NOTES

INTRODUCTION

1. Ken Sande, *The Peacemaker: A Biblical guide to Resolving Personal Conflict* (Grand Rapids: baker Publishing Group, 2006).

CHAPTER 1

1. *Romans 10:14-17 (KJV)*
2. *1 John 1:7 (KJV)*
3. *Romans 12:19 (KJV)*
4. *Ouoted at <u>http://www.brainyquote.com/quotes/quotes/r/</u>***rodneyking 445914***.<u>html</u> on March 23, 2015.*
5. *Layperson J. Telephone Interview, January 27, 2015.*

CHAPTER 2

1. Norman Shawchuck and Roger Heuser, *Managing the Congregation (Nashville Abingdon Press, 1996).*
2. *Clergy X. Telephone Interview, July 30, 2015.*

CHAPTER 3

1. *Mark 10:35-41 (KJV)*
2. *Clergy V. Personal Communication, July 29, 2015.*

CHAPTER 4

1. Quoted at <u>http://www.brainyquote.com/quotes/authors/s/stephen covey.html</u> on 1 March 2015.
2. *Matthew 6:33 (KJV)*
3. Clergy A. Telephone Interview, July 29 2015.

CHAPTER 5

1. Romans 8:28 (KJV)
2. Young Adult Layperson K. Personal Interview, August 2, 2015.

Dr. Willie Eugene Marshall is pastor of St. James African Methodist Episcopal Church family in St. Louis, MO. He is a mentor, leader, educator, counselor and a master encourager who has a heart for the people. Dr. Marshall enjoys family, preaching, traveling and empowering positive transformation in the lives of others. He is married to Kimberly Renee Huggins-Marshall. They are the proud parents of one son, Joshua James Huggins Marshall.

wekrm777@aol.com

www.optimisticexpectations.net

STAY POSITIVE

Printed in the United States
By Bookmasters